Living Tapestries

CHARLES H. NUMRICH

FAIRWAY PRESS

DRAWER L • LIMA, OHIO 45802

LIVING TAPESTRIES

Copyright © 1985 by
Fairway Press
Lima, Ohio

Tapestry designs made available by: Hmong Folk Art, Inc. Minneapolis, MN.;
Story Illustrations are rendered by Paul Sylvestre from Hmong tapestries;
Cover Photo by David Behr-Sylvestre of a Tapestry by Pa Le.

7561/ISBN 0-89536-939-7   PRINTED IN U.S.A.

Table of Contents

Introduction

Living Tapestries is a collection of legends and folk tales from the Hmong refugee community that has settled on the south side of Minneapolis. They represent art, culture, and verbal history from a people who have faced war, loss, and relocation as a regular part of their existence. These particular stories were gathered as part of a Theatre Unlimited project called "Images for Exiles," which was funded in 1982-83 by the Development Assistance Program Committee of the American Lutheran Church. Stories were collected from students of The Language Project, a non-profit English-as-a-Second-Language program, located at Our Saviour's Lutheran Church. "Images for Exiles" received a 1983 Public Art Award from the mayors of Minneapolis, St. Paul, Minnesota.

At a point in the history of the Hmong people when the younger generation is growing quickly into Western culture, the older people and the stories they learned as part of their heritage are often left behind and forgotten. These collected stories have been used as a teaching resource, to make a new language accessible through familiar images. Something of this culture that might have been lost in transition is now recorded for future generations, and for the rest of us who are learning to live with these most recent immigrants.

Many of the images in these stories are repeated over and over. The breakdown of this volume into types of stories is general, and it will be obvious that areas of concern overlap from section to section. It is clear that most of these stories have to do with loss and hope for future gain, usually in terms of beginning a family. It is in the gathered community and family that the Hmong feel most secure: through generations of passing on these stories they have maintained their unity.

There are many parallels with these tales in Biblical stories and other folk tales, and through telling them in a variety of settings, I have discovered that they have an almost universal appeal. These are stories to be told aloud; that is how they originated and how they have their deepest impact. By hearing them and considering them in relation to Hmong tapestries (the culture's other major art form), we can see an almost nomadic people who have carried their culture and history through years of loss and change, and who continue to cling to their identity in powerful images.

Our special thanks to Blong Moua, Lia Moua, Xeng Moua, and Xai

6

Neng Moua for all of their help, and to the members of The Language Project who shared their stories and their hopes with us.

Charles Numrich, Dramatist
Theatre Unlimited
Minneapolis, Minnesota

Section 1. Stories of loss and gain

Why There Are Rich Nations and Poor Nations

Long ago, when all things began, all people were the same: poor and hungry. They wandered through many empty lands and found very little food. As they came to the edge of the empty lands, they saw a beautiful, green garden, with a high stone fence around it. In the garden, they could see a tall tree, full of beautiful, ripe fruit. The people walked all around the wall to find a way into the garden. When they came to the gate, the gardener opened it and said, "Come in, all of you, and eat the fruit from my tree."

All the people rushed forward to get to the food. Some pushed harder than others, so they would be first. When the first group of people got to the tree, they picked up the fruit that was on the ground and began to eat as fast as they could. Much of the fruit was bad and rotten, but they were so hungry, they did not notice.

When the next group of people reached the tree, they found no fruit on the ground, so they picked it from the lowest branches and ate as much as they could. The people who came last found no fruit on the ground, or on the low branches. As they tried to reach the fruit high up in the tree, it fell off into their hands at the point of perfect ripeness, and they ate as much as they could.

So it is, the children of those who ate the poor fruit off the ground were poor for many generations. The children of those who ate the rich, ripe fruit were rich for many generations.

Xia Moo Pha and Ai Ka Lar

Xia Moo Pha and Ai Ka Lar were good friends. Xia Moo Pha had a very beautiful girl friend named E Na, and he visited her all the time.

Ai Ka Lar was very poor and never went anywhere. One day, Xia Moo Pha said to Ai Ka Lar, "Come with me tonight and we will visit E Na together." Ai Ka Lar said, "I would like to, but I am so poor, I have no clothes to wear." "I will loan you some clothes to wear," said Xia Moo Pha. So the two friends went to visit E Na.

When they got there, Xia Moo Pha went into the house and left Ai Ka Lar standing outside. Xia Moo Pha stayed inside for a long time, so Ai Ka Lar took out his "xim xuas" (a stringed instrument played with a bow) and began to play. E Na heard the music and said to Xia Moo Pha, "Go outside and bring in the person who is playing that beautiful, sad music." Xia Moo Pha went out and told Ai Ka Lar to come into the house, but Ai Ka Lar would not. When E Na heard this, she went out and asked Ai Ka Lar, "Why will you not come into my house?" Ai Ka Lar said, "I am so poor, I feel very shy with someone like you." E Na said, "Do not be shy; come in and we will talk." So Ai Ka Lar went inside.

As they were talking, E Na fell in love with Ai Ka Lar. Xia Moo Pha saw this and was very jealous. He told Ai Ka Lar to give him back the clothes he had loaned him. E Na said to Ai Ka Lar, "Give him back his clothes, I will give you other clothes to wear." They talked some more, then Xia Moo Pha and Ai Ka Lar left to go home. When they got home, Xia Moo Pha said, "We should travel to the merchant and buy some things together." Ai Ka Lar said, "I have no money to travel or to buy things." Xia Moo Pha said he would loan him some money, so Ai Ka Lar agreed to go along. The journey to the merchant would take a long time, so Ai Ka Lar went back to E Na to tell her he was leaving. He told her he would be back in three years and asked her to wait for him. E Na said she would wait.

On the way to the merchant, they went through a village and saw two snakes for sale. Xia Moo Pha said to Ai Ka Lar, "You should buy those two snakes," and gave him the money, so Ai Ka Lar bought the two snakes. In the next village, they saw two birds for sale and Xia Moo Pha said, "You should buy those birds, too," so Ai Ka Lar bought them. In the next village, they saw two dogs for sale and Xia Moo Pha said he should buy them, too, so Ai Ka Lar bought the two dogs. After that, all of Ai Ka Lar's money was gone.

Later, they traveled through a large forest far from home and got lost. Xia Moo Pha said, "You make a place for us to spend the night, and I will look for a way to get out of this forest." Xia Moo Pha knew the way out of the forest, so he left Ai Ka Lar there and went back home. He went to E Na and told her that Ai Ka Lar had been killed in a forest far from home and that he would be glad to marry her, now that Ai Ka Lar would never return. E Na said, "I told Ai Ka Lar that I would wait three years for him to return. I will wait that long; if he does not come back, I will marry you." So, they waited. When three years had passed, Xia Moo Pha went to E Na and said, "Today is the end of three years; now I will marry you." E Na said, "All right, but we should wait until tonight." That night as E Na and Xia Moo Pha prepared to be married, Ai Ka Lar returned. The dogs had led the way out of the forest, with the snakes alongside to make sure they went straight; and Ai Ka Lar rode on the backs of the two birds. He came home to E Na just in time to marry her.

The Wife and the Rich Man's Son
("Tus poj niam thiab neeg muaj nyiag tus tub")

Long ago, a young man and young woman got married. They lived together very happily, but the young man could find no work. One day, he heard that there was work in another country, far away. He told his wife he would go there to work and get money for them to live. He said he might be gone for three years and asked her to wait for him.

After the young man had been gone for some time, a rich man's son wanted the young wife for himself. He went to the young woman and said, "You are very beautiful. If you will let me touch your hand, I will pay you." The young woman said, "No, I am married." The rich man's son said, "I only want to touch your hand, and I will pay you well." The young woman thought about this and said, "Since you only want a touch, it will not be bad." So the rich man's son touched her hand and gave her the money.

The rich man's son came to see the young woman another day and said, "I want to marry you." The young woman said, "I have told you; I am already married." The rich man's son said, "But your husband is far away and you do not know if he will have any money when he comes home. If you marry me now, I will give you all the money you want." So the young woman agreed and they were married.

After three years, the young man returned to his home. When he heard that his wife had married the rich man's son, he took them both to court to get his wife back. In court, the judge asked whose wife she was; both the young man and the rich man's son claimed that she was his wife. The young woman did not say anything. The judge could not decide who was telling the truth, so he sent them to the temple, so the priests could decide.

The priests said they would find out who was telling the truth. There was a very large drum in the temple, and the priests said, "The man who can carry this drum around the temple three times is truly this woman's husband." Before this test, one of the priests was put inside the drum to make it very heavy. First the rich man's son and the young woman tried to carry the drum, but they could not go around the temple three times. When the young man saw that the rich man's son had failed, he said to his wife, "Hurry; help me; we must carry the drum around three times, then you will be my wife again." He picked up the drum with the young woman and hurried around the temple. The young woman was so tired from her first try that she was not much help. The young man kept telling her to hurry up. The young woman said, "I cannot go faster, but do not worry. When we finish carrying the drum, I will tell the priests that you are really my husband."

When they finished carrying the drum, the priest was let out of the drum and the young man, the rich man's son and the young woman were called to meet with the priests. The priest who had been inside the drum said, "Now we know who is telling the truth," because he had heard what the young woman had said. So the priests married the young man and young woman again, and the judge made the rich man's son pay damages to the young man.

The Man and His Two Wives
("Tus txiv thiab mws ob tug poj niam")

There once was a man with two wives who both gave birth to daughters at the same time. Very soon after that, the first wife died, leaving her daughter with a family who did not love her. The second wife, her daughter and the father made the first daughter work very hard all the time; she never had much to eat and could never go out and have fun. When the New Year came, the others went off to the celebration and left the first daughter at home to work. She was so sad that she cried out for her mother, "Where are you, mother? Why have you left me to live with these people who do not love me?" She looked for the suitcase that held her mother's clothes and, when she found it, she decided to put on her mother's best clothes and go to the party herself.

When she got to the party, she saw there were many people inside playing "istumen" (a ball game, played to music), so she stayed outside, away from the crowd. One young man inside saw her and went out to meet her. She saw this young man following her and she was afraid, so she ran home. She put her mother's clothes away and sat in front of the house in her own rags. When the young man came by the house, he asked her if she had seen a beautiful girl run past. She said she had not, but as he looked at her, he knew that she was the girl. He told her that she was very beautiful and stayed to talk with her in front of the house.

When the father, the second wife, and the second daughter

came home, the young man told them he thought this daughter was very beautiful and that he would like to marry her. The second wife did not like this and said, "I have a daughter who is even more beautiful. If you marry this one, you must marry my daughter too." The man said he would think about this, and the second wife invited him to stay for dinner so they could talk more.

The second wife prepared chicken and rice and, when they all sat down to eat, the young man said that he could not eat with the lights on. So the wife turned off the lights, and she put chicken and rice in front of the young man and her own daughter; but she put soybeans and an old bone in front of the first daughter. Before they could eat, the young man switched the daughters' plates, and the second daughter complained, "Mother, why did you give me soybeans and an old bone?" The mother said she had given her chicken and rice and, when she got up to turn on the lights, the young man switched the plates again and made the second daughter look very foolish.

When they finished eating, the mother insisted that the young man spend the night and sleep between the two daughters' beds. The man agreed and everyone went to bed. When the girls were asleep, the man switched their beds. A few minutes later the mother sneaked in to put something in the first daughter's eyes, so she would not wake up in the morning. Because the young man had switched the beds, she put it into her own daughter's eyes.

In the morning, the young man woke up very early and went away with the first daughter to marry her. The second daughter could not open her eyes, so she did not wake up. Later, when the mother came to see what had happened, she thought the young man had run off with her daughter and she was very happy. Then the girl rolled over and said, "Mother, I can't open my eyes," and the mother knew she had only tricked herself.

Section II. Stories about orphans

The Orphan Boy and the Chinese Man

Once there was a poor orphan boy. All he had was a cat, but it was a very special cat because it could sing. The boy and his cat were skinny, hungry and weak; they went from town to town begging. When the cat would sing, people would listen and laugh and toss them bones or old rice; and some even gave them money.

One day, the boy and his cat met a Chinese man on the road. The Chinese man wore a big hat and was leading a horse carrying goods to sell in the town. "Please, can you give us something," said the orphan boy. "Why should I," said the Chinese man, "I do not know you." The boy said, "If you give us something, my cat will sing for you." The cat began to sing beautifully, and the Chinese man listened. When the song ended, the man asked, "Is this your cat?" The boy answered, "Yes," and the Chinese man said, "I would give anything for a cat like that." The boy thought for a minute, then said, "Would you give your horse and all the things on it?" "Those are nothing," said the Chinese man. "I sell them and I buy more. This horse and I walk the same path every day and we get nowhere. I would gladly trade it all for that cat of yours." "And I will make that trade," said the orphan boy.

So, the orphan boy took the horse and all the goods, sold them in the town, and he was no longer poor. And the Chinese man went his way with a cat that could sing.

The Orphan Boy and the King of Heaven
(Tus me nyuam ntsuag thiab fuab tais)

A young orphan boy lived with his sister and her husband in a small house at the edge of the village. The boy loved to walk in the forest near the house. One day, when he was walking in the forest, a strange and beautiful bird flew over his head; then it fell to the ground and died. The boy had never seen a bird like this before and he was sad that it had died. He dug a small hole in the ground and buried the bird.

Earlier in the day, soldiers from the king of heaven had come to the village and told everyone that one of the king's daughters had changed into a strange and beautiful bird and had flown away. Anyone with news of such a bird would be rewarded by the king. When the orphan boy went home, he told his sister and her husband about the bird, and they asked him to show them where the bird was buried. They wondered if this bird might be the daughter of the king of heaven.

The boy dug up the bird's body and took it to the soldiers in the village. The boy, his sister, and her husband were taken at once to the king's palace. The king went to the boy and took the bird from his hands. When the king held the bird, its wings moved and it flew from his hands; then it turned into his beautiful daughter. She looked at her father and said, "Please let me die." "No," said her father, "I want you to live."

The daughter looked at the orphan boy and said, "He laid me

to rest so peacefully in the earth; please let me go back there."
"I will not," said her father; "Because of his kindness, you must
live." Then the king's daughter said, "Let the boy decide if I should
live or die." "Very well," said the king, turning to the boy, "You
will decide." The boy was afraid, but he said, "I think she should
live." "Then I will live," said the king's daughter.

The king of heaven was so happy, he offered to give the boy
any gift he wanted from the kingdom of heaven. The boy saw a
baby chick pecking in the dirt nearby and thought that it would
be nice to have a flock of chickens for himself. The boy said to
the king, "I would like that baby chick to start my own flock."
The king's face changed; his smile was gone. "No," said the king,
"any gift but that." The king's son stepped forward and said,
"Father, it is a fair gift for the life of one daughter." The boy did
not know why there was such a problem about one little chick,
but he knew he wanted it. At last, the king agreed and gave the
baby chick to the orphan boy, who promised to take good care
of it.

From that time on, the baby chick went everywhere with the
boy, but it did not grow. The boy did not get his flock of chickens,
but he found many things in the forest to sell in the village, and
his family was no longer poor. The boy always had new, clean
clothes to wear, even if his sister did not wash for him; and no
matter how early in the morning he got up to go to the forest,
there was always hot food for him to eat.

Still, the baby chick never changed and went everywhere with
him. It was with him one day when he went to help a widow in
the village and saved her life. The boy, who was now a young man,
married the widow, and they started their own family. Neither of
them ever had to cook or clean, and each of them thought the
other did all of the work. They did not know that it was the baby
chick who did all of their work for them, because the baby chick
was really the king of heaven's other daughter. So, the boy's gift
for saving the life of one daughter was to have the other daughter
serve him all of his life.

The Orphan Boy
("Yob nruag ntsuag")

There once was a poor orphan boy who lived in the west. He lost his land and his money and was forced to move to the east. He had nothing at all there and could find very little work. One day, when it was very hot, the boy went to the lake instead of looking for work. A group of children were playing in the water, and as they swam and laughed and played, one of the children drowned, but the others did not notice. When it got late, the children left the lake and the orphan boy went home. The parents of the child who drowned waited and waited, but she did not come home. When the father found out where his child had been, he went to the lake and began to look for her. Finally, he dove deep into the lake and found a dragon's village at the bottom. The father went to the first house in the village and asked the dragons if they had seen a little girl. The dragons said they had not, but they thought their neighbors had caught a deer that day.

When the father went to the next house, he did not see a deer, but his dead child. He was very angry, but he did not say anything to anyone. He went to the edge of the village, started a fire, and burned the village down. Then he swam to the surface and went home.

On another day when it was hot, the orphan boy did not look for work again; he went to sleep under a tree. A dragon came out of the tree, looking like an old man and asked the boy, "When will you go back home?" The orphan boy said that he was leaving in fifteen days. The dragon said, "When you get back to the west, tell the dragon of the west to come and help me rebuild my village, which was burned down."

The orphan boy went home in fifteen days and his sister held a party to welcome him. At the party, the boy was talking to a man about the lake behind their village. The boy asked, "Do you know about the dragon that lives in that lake?" The man said, "I have lived here all my life, and I know there is no dragon in that lake." After they argued for awhile, the orphan boy said, "Let's go call the dragon and we will see if it comes out." The man said, "If I call the dragon, it will come out and eat you up. If you call, it will come out and eat me up." Then the man thought for a minute and said, "I will call first."

The man stood at the edge of the lake and called and called, but no dragon came out of the lake. Then it was the orphan boy's turn. He stood at the edge of the lake and called, "Come out, dragon of the west. The dragon of the east has sent me to tell you that he needs your help to rebuild his village, which was burned down." The dragon came up out of the lake with its mouth open. The orphan boy jumped into the dragon's mouth and was taken to the dragon's home, deep in the lake. The dragon said to the boy, "You stay here and I will go help the dragon of the east. I will return in fifteen days. You must stay in this room and you must be very quiet, or there will be trouble." The orphan boy agreed to stay and the dragon left.

After ten days, the boy could not stand it and he cried out, "I am so lonely; why won't the dragon come back? I want to go home." The dragon's daughter was asleep in the next room and woke up at the sound of the boy's voice. She went to the door of the room and said, "My father told you to be quiet. You should do what he said, or there will be trouble." The next day the boy cried out again and woke the dragon's daughter. This time, she went in to see him and said, "When my father returns, he will want to give you something for the favor you have done him. He will offer you money, but you must say, 'Money is our tears.' Then he will offer you horses and cows, but you must tell him that you do not need any. When he asks what you do want, tell him that you would like his cat and his white umbrella."

The dragon returned at the end of fifteen days, and he thanked the orphan boy for the favor he had done. When he offered gifts, the orphan boy refused. Finally, he asked the boy what he wanted. The boy answered, "All I will need are your cat and your white umbrella." The dragon said, "Well, I have only one of each, but if you need them, they are yours." The orphan boy went back to the edge of the lake and slept under a tree with his cat and his white umbrella. When he woke up in the morning, the umbrella had turned into a beautiful house, and the cat was really the dragon's beautiful daughter. They lived there together with all they needed.

The Orphan Boy and the Bird
("Tsuag thiab noog")

There was once an orphan boy with no wife, who lived near an old couple. One day, as the old couple worked in the fields, they saw a beautiful girl swimming in the lake. When they saw the orphan boy later, they asked,

"Do you want to get married?" The orphan boy said, "I would like to get married, but I do not have a girl friend." The couple said, "If you want to find someone to marry, we will tell you what to do. Some afternoon, go down to the lake. There you will see a group of birds swimming in the water. On the shore of the lake, you will find the bird's wings. Take one pair of wings and hide them; then you will find someone to marry."

The next afternoon, the orphan boy went to the lake, and he did see a group of birds swimming in the water. On the shore, he found the wings where the birds had left them. He took one pair of wings and hid them in the forest. When the birds were done swimming, they came to the shore and put on their wings. One of the birds could not find her wings, and the others flew off and left her behind. As she looked for her wings, she saw the orphan boy, who asked her, "Where are you going?" The bird said, "I cannot find my wings, and the others have gone home and left me. Have you seen my wings?" The orphan boy said, "No, I have not. Why don't you stay at my house tonight and we can come back to the lake tomorrow. If your friends are here then, they can take you home." The bird agreed and stayed at the orphan boy's house that night. The next day, they went back to the lake, but her friends did not return, so she could not go home.

The bird stayed with the orphan boy and they were married. They lived together for four years and had two children. The mother went off to work every day, and the father stayed home to take care of the children. When the children were unhappy, the father took his wife's wings down from the ceiling where they were hidden, put them on, and flew around the room until the children laughed. One day the father had to go to work, and the mother stayed home. All day the children cried and pointed to the ceiling. Nothing their mother did could make them happy, and she wondered why they pointed to the ceiling. Then she looked up and saw her wings, hanging from the ceiling. She took her wings down, put them on, and flew back to her home, leaving her children and her husband behind.

When the husband came home from work, he found that his wife and her wings were gone. He left the children with the old couple and went to look for his wife. He walked and walked, until he came to the edge of the ocean, but there was no way for him to cross it. He met an old man there who asked the orphan boy what he wanted. He told the old man that his wife was a bird, that she had found her hidden wings and gone home, and that he was going to find her. The old man said, "She has crossed the ocean to her home and you will never cross it by yourself. You must go to the big tree where there are two eagles. Climb the tree and hide under the wing of one of the eagles. They will fly you to the bird country and you will find your wife there." The orphan boy did as the old man had told him and flew away to the bird country with the eagles.

When the orphan boy got to the bird country, he walked all around trying to find his wife. Near a river, he saw a young girl putting water in a bucket. He went to her and asked if she had seen his wife. When he told her what his wife looked like, the young girl said, "I am sorry to tell you this, but your wife is marrying someone else today. I am getting water to take to her wedding party." The orphan boy put his wedding ring into the girl's bucket and said, "Take this to my wife and ask her to drink from it first"

The girl took the bucket, and when the wife drank from it, she saw her husband's wedding ring in the bottom. She told her father and mother that she could not get married because her husband was waiting for her near the river. Her parents were angry with her because the party had begun, and the man who wanted to marry her had already paid. Her parents told her to bring her husband to them, so they could figure out what to do.

The orphan boy and the other man met with the parents, and her father said, "You both want to marry my daughter, so we must have a contest to decide. I will divide my field in half and each of you will work on a half. The man who finishes first will marry my daughter." The two men went to work, and the orphan boy finished first. The father said, "You will marry my daughter, but this man has already paid, so you must pay him back," which the orphan boy did. Then the wife's father asked where they would live and the orphan boy said they would go back home to their children. The father said, "Well, my daughter is a bird, so she can fly back to your home; but you cannot. I will help you. Go to the forest and cut some wood, then bring it to me." The orphan boy did this, and his wife's father made him an airplane, so he could fly back to his home.

Section III. Stories of transformation

The Tiger and the Farmer
The Elephant Gives Up Its Wisdom
Tuam Los Pej and Xyuam Lis Koo
The Man With Three Wives
The King and His Seven Sons

The Tiger and the Farmer
("Tsov thiab tus neeg ua teb")

A farmer and his family lived far out in the country and all of their neighbors lived very far away from them. Every day, the farmer's wife and his daughter worked in their small house and garden, and the farmer worked in the fields near the forest. One day as the farmer sat down to eat his lunch, a tiger attacked and killed him. The tiger ate the farmer, then put on the farmer's hat and coat and changed himself into the farmer. He went to the farmer's house, and the farmer's wife and daughter thought he was the farmer. The wife cooked supper and they all sat down to eat.

After the meal, the farmer's daughter climbed the ladder into the loft where she slept, and the farmer's wife went to bed. When it was very late and they were asleep, the tiger took off the farmer's hat and coat and changed back into the tiger. He attacked the farmer's wife in her bed and she screamed for help. The daughter woke up and called down from the loft, "Who is down there? What's happening?" The tiger went to the bottom of the ladder in the darkness and said, "It's me, your father; come down and see."

"No," said the daughter, "it's too dark and I am afraid; you come up here." "All right," said the tiger, and he started to climb the ladder. When the daughter saw that he used four legs to climb instead of two, she knew it was not her father, but a tiger. She opened a jar of red-hot pepper that was stored in the loft and threw it into the tiger's eyes. The tiger screamed in pain and fell back down the ladder. The girl shouted for help, and there was so much noise, even the neighbors from far away heard and came running to help. They ran into the house, killed the tiger, and saved the girl.

'The Elephant Gives Up Its Wisdom
("Tus ntxhw muab nws gehov kev xaj laj")

A very poor woman with no husband lived near the forest. One day as she was walking in the forest, she got very thirsty. On the path an elephant had left its footprint in the ground, and water had settled there. The woman drank some of the water, and then she went home. Months later, the people in the village saw that the woman was pregnant, but no one knew who the baby's father was.

This woman had a son, who grew up to be wise and lucky and strong. When his friends asked who his father was, the boy always said it was the elephant that lived in the forest. The elephant did not want to give its wisdom to other elephants; it wanted to help people. When the boy became a man, he was king of his people and led them with the strength, luck, and wisdom of the elephant.

(Other stories are told that when an elephant meets an orphan, it will give up its trunk to be made into a wife or husband for the orphan, so they can start a new family.)

Tuam Los Pej and Xyuam Lis Koo

A young boy named Tuam Los Pej and a young girl named Xyuam Lis Koo lived in the same village and walked to school together every day. One day as they were walking home, they saw two birds in a tree talking to each other. Xyuam Lis Koo asked, "Do you know what they are saying?" Tuam Los Pej listened to the birds and said, "The male bird says, 'Cheng, cheng, cheng.'" Xyuam Lis Koo said, "You do not understand them." As they walked through the village, they saw two chickens talking to each other. Xyuam Lis Koo asked,

"Do you know what they are saying?" The boy listened and said, "The male chicken says, 'Bawk, bawk, bawk,' and the female chicken says 'Bawk, bawk, bawk.'" The girl said, "You do not understand them either."

The boy and the girl came to the place in the road where they parted to go to their own homes. Xyuam Lis Koo knew that she was to marry someone else that night and never see Tuam Los Pej again. She said to him, "You do not understand the birds or chickens, and you will not understand what I will say to you. When you do understand, it will be too late, and you will be sad. Goodbye." Then the boy and the girl went to their homes.

The next day, Tuam Los Pej went to school, but Xyuam Lis Koo was not there. He went to her house after school, and her mother told him that Xyuam Lis Koo had gone away to marry someone else. Tuam Los Pej was very sad; he went to all the places he had been with Xyuam Lis Koo and he cried. "You were right, Xyuam Lis Koo. I understand too late, and I am sad. Now I will die for love." Then Tuam Los Pej died.

When Xyuam Lis Koo heard this, she went to his house and asked to see the boy's grave. They took her to the grave where she cried and cried. When her tears touched the ground, the grave opened up and she jumped into the coffin. The grave closed up and she was gone. When her husband heard about this, he went to the grave with his neighbors to see what had happened. He told his friends to dig up the grave and get his wife; but when they dug, there was nothing to be found. Xyuam Lis Koo's husband went home, very sad.

One of the husband's neighbors, an old man, had left his pipe at the grave and went back to get it. At the grave, he heard voices, like two people talking. He ran back to the husband and told him to dig up the grave again. This time, the boy and girl had turned into two stones. The husband was very angry and told his friends to put the two stones on opposite sides of the river, so his wife could never be with Tuam Los Pej again. So the river ran between Tuam Los Pej and Xyuam Lis Koo.

The next day the husband and his friends went back to the river and found that the two stones had changed into two large trees, and their branches were joined together over the river. The husband was angry and told his friends to cut the trees down and burn them, so his wife could never be with Tuam Los Pej again. In the fire from the two trees, Tuam Los Pej and Xyuam Lis Koo changed into butterflies and flew up to heaven, where they are with each other forever.

The Man and His Three Wives
("Tus txiv neej thiab nws peb tug poj niam")

There was a man with three wives, who told them he was going to another country to find work. He said that he might be gone for four years, and that they should wait for him. When he left, all three of his wives were pregnant.

Soon after he left, the man's first wife gave birth to a son; the second and third wives gave birth to daughters. The second and third wives thought their husband would love the first wife best because she had a son, so they decided to kill the boy. They took the baby, covered him with salt, and put him in the field where the man's cow was feeding, and the cow ate him. Then the second and third wives put a rock in the first wife's throat, so she could not tell anyone what happened.

Four years later, the husband returned. His second and third wives told him they had given birth to daughters. When he asked about the first wife, they told him she had not given birth and now she could not talk. Soon after the man returned, his cow gave birth to a male calf. As the calf grew up, it followed the man to work every day and helped him. He began to wonder why the calf was so helpful, and he mentioned it to his wives. The second and third wives were afraid that this calf was really the baby boy who had been killed by the cow, so they decided on a plan to kill the calf.

The next day, the third wife told her husband that she was very sick and he should get a "suab" to help her. (The "saub" [pronounced "show"] is a person who is very good at healing.) The husband went out to the road and burned a piece of rice paper and called for help, "My third wife is sick; can anyone help me?" The second wife was hiding behind a rock, and she changed her voice and answered him, "You must kill your male calf, then your third wife will get better." The man did not know it was his second wife speaking, so he went to the field to kill the calf.

When the man saw the calf, he was sad to think about killing it. "You have loved me and helped me so much, I wish I did not have to kill you. But I must, so my third wife will get better." When the calf heard this, he ran away and lived with the cows in the king of heaven's field.

One day the calf saw the king's daughter walking past the field. She was very beautiful, and he wanted to see her again. One night, he went to the chicken coop, took off the calf's skin, and changed into a young man. He went to the king's daughter and told her he loved her. She asked who he was and where he came from. The young man said, "I live with your father's cows," but she did not believe him. The young man stayed with the king's daughter all night. In the morning, he went back to the chicken coop, put on the calf's skin, and joined the cows in the king's field. After that, the young man went to visit the king's daughter every night.

One day, she told her father about this young man and the king said, "Tonight, when the young man is asleep, go to the chicken coop. If you find a calf's skin there, hide it." That night, the daughter did what her father had told her to do. In the morning, the young man went to the chicken coop, but could not find his calf's skin. The king's daughter found him there and took him to the king.

The king asked the young man who he was and where he had come from. The young man told the story of what had happened to him and then told the king, "I love my father, and I would like to live with him, but his second and third wives know who I am and they will try to kill me again." "Well," said the king, "then you can stay here and marry my daughter, and some day you will be king in my place."

Years later, the young man returned to earth to see his father and mother. He told his father who he was and what had happened. His mother still could not talk, but when the young man hit her in the throat, the rock came out and she could tell her husband the truth. The husband and the first wife were very happy to have their son back, and he decided to take them to the kingdom of heaven with him. The second and third wives said they would like to go too. The young man told them that he would take his father and mother first and then he would come back for them. He did take his mother and father to the kingdom of heaven, but he never returned, and the other two wives are still waiting.

The King and His Seven Sons
("Huab tais thiab nws xya leej tub")

Once there was a king on earth who had seven sons, and there was a king in heaven who had no sons. The king of heaven was very old, and he sent a letter to the king of earth saying, "I am too old to be king. Send me one of your sons to be king in my place." The king of earth asked his sons which one of them would like to go. The first son said, "I will go to be king of heaven." So the father gave him a horse and sent him on his way. As the first son was traveling, his father changed into a tiger and attacked him. The first son was frightened by the tiger and he rode back home. Then the king went to each of his sons and asked if they wished to be king of heaven. Each of them went off on the horse; each was attacked by the tiger and each rode back home, too frightened to go on.

Finally, the king came to his seventh son and asked if he would like to be king of heaven. The seventh son said he would, and he was sent off on the horse. On the road, the father changed into a tiger and attacked. The seventh son did not run away; he jumped off the horse, pulled out his knife and attacked the tiger. The tiger ran away and the seventh son continued his journey. Later, a snake tried to attack him, but he chased it away with his knife too. Then a bear tried to attack, and the son chased it away too.

The king watched his son's bravery and came to him on the road. "You are wise and brave, my son; you will make a very good king of heaven." Then he gave his son rice and water for the trip and warned him, "Do not share your food with anyone, or you will go hungry on your journey." As the son traveled, he saw a man begging for food. "If you will only give me food and water," he said, "I will be your slave and go everywhere with you." The son shared his food with the man and the man became his slave. Before they reached the kingdom of heaven, the food ran out, and the man took the horse and made the son his slave.

When they reached heaven, the man told the king that he was the son of the king of earth. So the beggar man was made king of heaven and the seventh son of the king of earth had to serve him as a slave. One day, the son saw some bees and ants who were in trouble, and he helped them. When they saw how sad the boy was, they asked what was wrong. He told them his story, and they said they would help. "Go to the old king," they told him, "and tell him the truth. We will make sure everything works out right."

The son went to the old king and told him that he was the true son of the king of the earth, but the old king did not know who was telling the truth. To test them, the king dumped a bag of rice and a bag of soybeans on the floor and said, "Whoever can separate the rice from the soybeans will be king in my place." The beggar could not do it, but the son went to the ants, who came and separated the rice and soybeans into piles for him. Then the king said, "I need some honey. Whoever brings honey will be king in my place." The beggar looked everywhere, but he could find no honey. But the son went to the bees and they gave him all the honey he wanted. So the old king knew the boy was the seventh son of the king of earth. And he made him king of heaven, with the beggar as his slave.

Section IV. Stories about animals

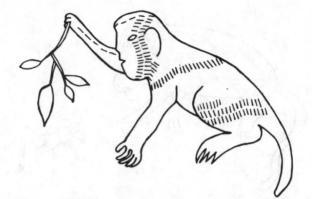

When All The Animals Were Refugees
("Thaum tsiaj yog neeg thoj nam")

When the world began, it was dry desert everywhere and it was very hard for all the animals to find enough food and water. A group of monkeys lived in the desert, and every day the men would go to look for food and water. Often, they would find nothing. One day, all the men went to look for food, leaving the women and children behind. They traveled very far in the desert and, by evening, they had found very little food. They decided not to go back home, so they rested there for the night. The next day, they went farther into the desert, and again they found very little food. That night they were too far away to go back home, so they rested, and the next day they went farther into the desert.

After many days of looking, they found a place with food and water and many trees. They were happy because life was good there, but none of them could remember how to get back to their families. They climbed into the tall trees and called out into the desert for their families to join them, but the women and children were too far away to hear them.

At last, they joined with the other monkeys there and started new families. Still every morning, these monkeys climb into the trees and call into the desert, hoping their families will hear them. At the same time, their new wives sit on the ground and hum and purr, as if to say, "They will never hear you; they will never come; we are glad that you will stay here with us."

The Grasshoppers and the Monkeys
("Koog thiab liab")

Once, there was a large group of grasshoppers, thousands and thousands, who lived near the forest. A group of monkeys came out of the forest and saw the grasshoppers. The big monkeys said to the little grasshoppers, "Do you want to fight?" The grasshoppers were afraid, and they said to the monkeys, "We will fight with you, but we must wait for grandmother to bring the red blanket." The monkeys laughed at this and said, "You are afraid to fight with us!" The grasshoppers said, "We will fight, but first we must wait for grandmother to bring the red blanket." The monkeys laughed again and went away.

Before the monkeys got back to the forest, it got dark, so they slept on the cold, hard ground. The grasshoppers all slept together in the grass and stayed warm all night. In the morning, the sun came up and the sky turned red. The grasshoppers warming up faster than the stiff, cold monkeys attacked by the thousands and chased the monkeys back into the forest. Then the grasshoppers thanked the sun (Grandmother) for her warmth (the red blanket), and for making the little grasshoppers stronger than the big monkeys.

The Tiger and the Wildcat
("Tus tsov thiab tus plis")

There was once a herd of goats, and the male goats took the baby goats to feed on the grass in the fields. When they came back, the female goats said, "You should keep them in the fields longer; they are still hungry." The male goats said, "You take them out to the fields tomorrow and bring them back when you want to." The next day the female goats took the baby goats out and kept them in the fields until it was almost dark, and they got lost on their way home. The herd went to sleep in a strange place and a wildcat saw them. The wildcat did not know what kind of animals they were, but he could tell they would be good to eat. He found a tiger, and they went off to catch one of these animals.

One of the female goats woke up as the tiger and the wildcat got close. When she stood up to face them, the tiger said, "What kind of animal are you? And what is that hanging down between your back legs?" The female goat said, "We are goats, and that is my udder, which the great spirit gave me to smother tigers and wildcats." This scared the tiger and the wildcat, and they ran away as fast as they could.

The tiger ran much faster and had to keep telling the wildcat to hurry up. Then the tiger stopped and tied their tails together. "Now you will have to run as fast as I do," said the tiger and he ran away. The tiger ran so fast that he dragged the wildcat along the ground and killed him. The wildcat's lips drew back over his teeth, so, even though he was dead, he looked as if he was smiling. When the tiger looked back at the wildcat, he said, "Hurry up; this is no time to be laughing." Then the tiger looked back at the wildcat again and said, "Stop smiling at me!" The tiger ran faster, and it still looked as if the wildcat was smiling. Finally the tiger stopped running and shouted, "Why are you smiling?" Then he saw that the wildcat was dead.

The tiger dug a hole and buried the wildcat. Then he jumped up onto a rock, and the wildcat's body jumped out of the hole on top of him. The tiger dug a deeper hole and buried the wildcat, but when he jumped up on the rock, the wildcat's body jumped on top of him again. So the tiger dug an even deeper hole and buried the wildcat again. He jumped up on the rock, and the wildcat's body jumped on top of him again.

"Well," said the tiger, "if you don't want to stay buried, I will have to eat you." So the tiger ate and ate, until only the tip of the wildcat's tail was left. The tiger took one last big bite and screamed in pain. It was then that the tiger realized their tails were still tied together. He untied their tails, buried the wildcat and that was the end of that.

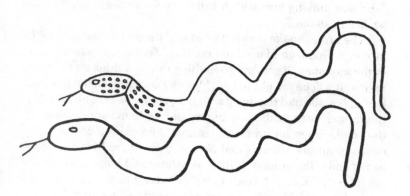

The Gift From the Snake
("Khov khoom ua nab muab.")

A farmer lived near the mountains with his wife and three daughters. Every day he went to the mountain to work. One day the farmer was walking home, and he saw a green female snake and a yellow male snake, tangled up in the road, making love. The farmer was afraid of snakes, so he threw his knife at them. The yellow snake got away, but the green snake had the tip of her tail cut off as she went into the ground. When the green snake went home, her husband asked what had happened to her tail. She told him the farmer had cut it off while she was on the road. Her husband, a brown snake, went off to the farmer's house for revenge.

When the farmer got home, he told his wife what had happened; he was afraid there would be trouble because he cut off the snake's tail. The farmer's wife told him to sit down and eat and not worry about it, but he kept pacing up and down, worrying about what might happen to him. Meanwhile, the brown snake wrapped his tail around the farmer's chimney and let his head hang down in front of the door. The farmer heard a noise at the door and when he opened it, he saw the head of the large brown snake. "What do you want," asked the farmer. "You cut off my wife's tail," said the snake, "and now I will kill you." The farmer said, "I did cut off a snake's tail, but it could not have been your wife." "Why not," asked the snake. "Because" said the farmer, "she was making love with a yellow snake in the road; he must be her husband."

The brown snake realized what had happened and said to the farmer, "Thank you for telling me this. Tomorrow, when you go to the mountain, if you find something to eat or drink on the road, take it; it will be my gift to you." When the brown snake got back home, his wife had run away with the yellow snake. The next day, the farmer went to the mountain, and he found some water on the road. When he drank this water, he could understand the words of all the animals and he could see everything that happened under the ground. When the farmer told his wife about the gift from the snake, she did not believe him. For one year, he told everyone about his gift, but no one would believe him.

At that time, the king was having trouble with ants. They began to crawl under the palace and into the basement. There were so many ants no one could get rid of them, and no one could tell the king why they were there. Then someone remembered hearing about the farmer who could understand animals, so the king sent for him. The farmer stood outside the palace and listened to the ants. Then he went to the king and said, "The ants have come because you have some very good liquor brewing in your basement and they want it. They have told ants all over the country, and now they will all come to taste your liquor." It was true that the king was brewing liquor in the basement, but no one knew about it. When the liquor was taken away, the ants left, but the king did not really believe the farmer could understand the animals.

Later the king had another problem with animals and he sent for the farmer again. There was a bird's nest in a tree outside the king's bedroom. The baby birds cried and made noise all the time, and the king could not sleep. The farmer came and listened to the birds, then said to the king, "There are nine baby birds in the nest, and they are crying because there is not enough room for all of them. Some are being crushed in the bottom and want to get out."

The king still did not believe the farmer could understand the animals, so the farmer said, "I can tell you something that will prove it to you. When the parents of these baby birds made their nest, they looked everywhere for things to make it strong. They went to the river and pulled one long hair from the dragon's beautiful daughter and put it into their nest." The king had the nest taken down and the baby birds put in a larger place. When he took the nest apart, he found one long, beautiful hair from the dragon's daughter, and the king finally believed that the farmer could understand the animals.

(This is only the first section of a story which the teller said "never ends.")

Section V. Stories about ghosts

How Sickness Came To Earth
("Vim li cas mob thiaj los rau ntiaj teb")

Before the earth began, a man and a woman, who were brother and sister, lived in the sky. Their first children were a boy, Lu Tu, and a girl, Gao Tse, who learned how to make music and dance. Then the man and the woman had other children. There were two boys: Teng Chu, the older, held up the sky, and Lolo Chu, the younger, caused lightning and rain. Their last child was an egg. The man and the woman waited three years for the egg to hatch, but nothing happened. So they broke open the egg to see what was inside. Many, many people came from the egg, and they spread out over the earth. There were so many people that they had to be given last names.

The man who lived in the sky looked at all of his children and said, "We have made many people to live on earth; we have children who make music and dance and children who support the sky and bring lightning and rain. We have done enough." Then the man and his sister died and went to earth to be human. He took the name Mon Yalu.

Later, Lolo Chu's wife had children which were also eggs. They waited for nine years, but the eggs did not hatch. Lolo Chu sent a message to earth to ask his father what to do. Mon Yalu returned to heaven and looked at the eggs. "Before I was born on earth," he said, "your mother gave birth to eggs, and there were people inside. These eggs do not have people inside; they are filled with evil spirits which will make people sick and die. To save the people of earth, you should burn these eggs."

Lolo Chu said, "These eggs are my children; they are like my heart; I will keep them." Mon Yalu went back to earth, and one year later, the eggs hatched. The evil spirits came out of the eggs and chased Lolo Chu and his wife all over heaven, trying to eat them. His wife could not escape and she was eaten, but Lolo Chu flew away to earth and was saved. "I cannot have this," said Lolo Chu; "I will make a hole in the sky so the spirits will go to earth and leave me alone." Lolo Chu cut a hole in the sky, and the evil spirits went to earth, and people got sick and died for the first time.

To help the people, Gao Tse went to earth and taught them voodoo, so they could heal sickness, and Lu Tu taught people to sing and play instruments at the funerals of those who died.

The Mother and Her Son
("Tus niam thiab nws tus tub")

A mother and her son lived in a small house on the edge of the village. They were very poor and the boy set traps in the forest to catch animals. Every morning he would check his traps to see if he had caught anything. One day there was a tiger caught in one of his traps. The tiger begged the boy not to kill him, "If you let me live, I will help you whenever you need help." So the boy let the tiger go free.

Another day the boy found a wildcat caught in one of his traps. The wildcat begged the boy not to kill him, "If you let me live, I will help you whenever you need help." So the boy let the wild-cat go free. Another day, the boy found a ghost caught in his trap. The ghost also said, "If you let me live, I will help you whenever you need help." So, the boy let the ghost go free, and the ghost went home with him.

The ghost lived with the boy for a long time and helped him find a wife. Later, the king saw the boy's wife and she was so beautiful the king wanted her for himself. The king said to the boy, "We will have a cock-fight. If my rooster wins, I will take your wife. If your rooster wins, you will be king in my place." When the boy heard this, he cried, but the ghost said, "Do not cry; the wildcat said he would help you. Go to him for help now." So the boy went to the forest to find the wildcat, and the wildcat said he would help.

The wildcat changed into a rooster and went with the boy to fight the king's rooster. When they were fighting, the boy's rooster changed back into the wildcat and killed the king's rooster. The king was very angry and said to the boy, "You may keep your wife, but I cannot let you be king right now; you will have to wait." The king went home, and the ghost followed him. When he got home, the king had a meeting with the snake and the spirit-eagle to find out which one of them could get the boy's wife for him. The ghost listened to all that was said at the meeting.

"I can get this woman for you," said the snake. "How will you do it?" asked the king. "I will hide in the woodpile and when she gets wood to start a fire, I will bite her and bring her back to you." So the king sent the snake to get the boy's wife for him. The ghost returned to the boy's home and warned him not to let his wife make the fire in the morning. The next day, the ghost went out and started a big fire. Then he pulled the snake out of the wooodpile, threw it into the fire, and killed it.

When the snake did not return, the king asked the spirit-eagle if he could get the boy's wife. The spirit-eagle said, "I will fly high up in the sky and call her name. The first time I call her face will turn yellow; the second time I call her face will turn more yellow; the third time I call she will follow me back to you." So the king sent the spirit-eagle to get the boy's wife for him. The spirit-eagle flew high in the sky and called the woman's name. The first time he called her face turned yellow; the second time it turned more yellow and the third time her spirit left her body and followed the spirit-eagle back to the king. The boy was left with only his wife's dead body and he started to cry. The ghost said, "Do not cry; just hold her hand and wait; I will bring her spirit back."

The ghost cut some pieces of bamboo and went to the king's house, where there was a party for the king's new wife. The ghost sat outside the house and started to weave a basket with the pieces of bamboo. The spirit-eagle came outside and asked what he was doing. The ghost said, "I have to take a chicken home, so I am weaving a basket to carry it." The spirit-eagle said, "That basket is no good; any chicken could get out of it." The ghost said, "Will you get into the basket and show me how a chicken could get out?" The spirit-eagle got into the basket, but he could not get out. When the ghost had him trapped, he said, "Tell me how you got the boy's wife to follow you to the king." The spirit-eagle told him, and the ghost asked, "What gives you the power to do that?" The spirit-eagle said, "My black tongue."

The ghost said to the spirit-eagle, "You must bring this woman back to her husband, or I will kill you." So the spirit-eagle called the woman three times again, and her spirit returned to her body and she came back to life in her own house. "Now," said the ghost, "show me this black tongue which gives you so much power." When the spirit-eagle stuck out his tongue, the ghost cut it off so it could never have power over people again; then he let the spirit-eagle go free. When the ghost returned to the boy's home, he saw that everything was fine; he had paid his debt to the boy for sparing his life, so the ghost went off to live somewhere else.

Separating People and Spirits
("Cais neej thiab cais dab")

Long ago there was an old man who was a merchant. One night he told his wife that he would leave the next day to go to another country on business. If there were things for him to buy, he would be gone for three years. If there was no business, he would be gone for only three months. A spirit was outside the house who heard what the old man said to his wife and watched as the old man left the next morning. Three months later the spirit changed himself to look like the old man and went to his home. He told the wife there had been no business in the other country, so he had come home early. The spirit looked just like the old man, so the wife did not realize anything was wrong. The spirit stayed with the woman and lived with her as her husband.

At the end of three years, the real old man came back with a cow and horse he had bought in the other country. When he went into his house, he saw the other old man and asked his wife who it was. She said it was her husband, but the old man said, "I am your husband." They looked alike, so she did not know which one to believe. The spirit said, "Remember, I told you if there was no business I would come back in three months." "No," said the old man, "there was business, so I stayed three years. You can see the cow and the horse I have brought home." The two old men argued, but they could not convince the wife which one was telling the truth. Then they took the case to the king, who told them it would take him one year to decide who was telling the truth. So they all went home to wait for the king to decide.

A few days later, two students were walking by the king's house on their way to a cock-fight. As they went by, the king spit on them. The students stopped, and when they saw who had spit on them, they said, "We have heard all about the case of the two old men which will take you a year to decide. We could find out the truth in three days." The king said, "I have been king for many years and I have never seen a case like this. The two old men look exactly alike. You could never decide which one is the real husband." The students said, "If we can find out which is the real husband, will you let our decision stand?" The king said, "If you can find the truth in that case, you deserve to be kings in my place." The students said, "We will do it. Bring the three people here in three days."

The students went home and cut a piece of bamboo. They hollowed it out and, three days later, took it to the king's house. When the three people arrived, the students said, "Both men will try to crawl through this piece of bamboo. The one that can crawl from one end to the other is the real husband of this woman." The spirit said, "I can do that; I will go first," and he crawled right through the little piece of bamboo. Then the old man tried, but he could not fit into the piece of bamboo. "So," said the king, "what is your decision?" The students said, "We are not sure yet. First we have to tie up these two old men; then we will know for sure." When the old men were tied up, the students said, "Now we can tell you. The one who could crawl through the bamboo is not the real husband." "How do you know," asked the king. The students said, "We know that no two people on earth look exactly the same; and we know that a real person could not crawl through such a small piece of bamboo; and we know that a spirit can change itself to look like any person. We tricked the spirit into crawling through the bamboo; then we tied both of them up so the spirit could not get away." The students untied the old man and said, "This is the woman's husband."

The king knew that the students were right, and he sent the old man home with his wife. He made the students kings in his place, and they killed the spirit. Since that time, spirits have been forced to live separated from real people.

Xee Xai and Ma Nai

There was once a king with seven wives. His first wife had two sons, Xee Xai and Ma Nai, but the king did not love them and sent them away to live in the forest. A "saub" found the boys in the forest and took them to a place where they could live and study with him. The two boys lived and studied and hunted in the forest.

One day, Ma Nai was sleeping and Xee Xai went hunting alone. He saw a deer and started to chase it. The deer was really a wild ghost, who had changed himself into a deer. Xee Xai chased the deer over four or five mountains, but then he lost sight of it. Suddenly, he saw a man coming toward him who was very angry. "Why are you chasing me?" asked the man; "I am a poor hunter looking for food, just like you." Xee Xai said, "I was not chasing you. I was chasing a deer." They began to argue back and forth; they fought and chased each other up into the sky.

Their fighting made the whole earth shake and woke up Ma Nai. He took his chain and went to see what was happening. Ma Nai's chain had the power to prove a person's honesty and it would tie up anyone who was lying. Ma Nai threw his chain up into the sky and caught the man fighting with Xee Xai. He pulled him back to earth, and when the man hit the ground, he changed into the wild ghost. The wild ghost begged the two brothers, "Please do not kill me. Let me go free. I did not mean to cause trouble. I will leave you alone if you only let me go." Ma Nai said to him, "We will let you go free, but you must leave here forever. If we see you again, we will kill you." So they let the wild ghost free and it went to live in another part of the country.

On another day, some time later, Xee Xai went hunting alone again, and he saw another hunter in the forest. The hunter asked him who he was, and Xee Xai told him that he and his brother were sons of the king, but they were forced to live in the forest. The hunter said, "I am so glad I've found you. You must go back to your home and save your sister." "What has happened to her?" asked Xee Xai. The hunter told him that a wild ghost had appeared in the village and demanded payment from the people. One person from each house had to be given to the wild ghost each day, or he threatened to destroy the village. "Very soon," said the hunter, "the wild ghost will get your sister. If you love her, you must go home and save her."

Xee Xai and Ma Nai told the "saub" that they had to go home to save their sister, but they would return to him as soon as they could. When they got to the village, they saw a small house on top of the hill. This was the house where people were taken for the wild ghost. They found their sister sitting in the house and they took her away. Then Xee Xai sat in the house and Ma Nai hid close by with his chain. When the wild ghost flew into the village from the ends of the earth, Ma Nai threw his chain and tied him up again. Xee Xai and Ma Nai sent their sister home and went back into the forest. When their sister got home, her parents were still crying for her, but she said, "Do not cry; I have come back alive." Her parents asked how this had happened, and she told them her two brothers had saved her. When they asked who the brothers were, she told them "Xee Xai and Ma Nai," and her parents cried for joy. They went to the forest and took the two brothers home. Xee Xai and Ma Nai were so wise and brave that their father made them kings in his place.

Section VI. Stories about brothers

The Story of the Two Brothers
The Older Brother and the Younger Brother
The Two Brothers and the Fish
The Dragon and the Two Brothers
The Three Brothers
The Father and His Three Sons

The Story of the Two Brothers
("Zaj dab neeg ob kwv tej")

Once there were two brothers whose parents had died. Soon after the death of the parents, the older brother got married and his wife did not like having the younger brother around. They wanted the younger brother to work in the fields with them, but they did not want him to live in their house. So the younger brother slept each night on his father's grave and worked in the fields every day. A tree began to grow out of the father's grave, and, when it was big enough, the younger brother used this tree for his house.

One night while he was sleeping in the tree, he dreamed that if he kicked the tree just right, money would come out of it. The next day, he kicked the tree as he had in his dream, and money did come out of it. He took all of this money to a cave and stayed there many days counting it. The older brother began to wonder where his brother was and he sent his wife to look for him. She went to the tree that grew from the father's grave, but she did not find him there. Finally, she found the cave, and saw the younger brother inside, counting money. She picked up one of the coins and went back to her husband.

"I found your brother," she said. "He is in a cave near your father's grave and he has lots of money." The older brother followed his wife to the cave and went in to see for himself. He found his younger brother there and asked, " Where did you get all of this money?" The younger brother told him that it had come from the tree that grew on their father's grave. "I need money too," said the older brother, "how do I get money from this tree?" The younger brother told him how to kick the tree so money would come from it. "You must only kick it three times," warned the younger brother, "if you kick it more than that, it will be very bad."

The older brother went to the tree and kicked it once; money came from it; he kicked it again and more money came from it. Then he said to his wife, "This is the third time. I will kick it as hard as I can so I will have more money than my brother." He kicked the tree as hard as he could, but instead of money, stew fell from the tree, all over him. The older brother was very angry, so he took an ax, cut the tree down, and went home. When the younger brother came back and saw that his tree had been cut down, he went to his brother and asked what had happened. The older brother said, "The tree was no good, so I cut it down. When I kicked it, stew came out of the tree and got me all wet."

The younger brother was very sad, and he went back to his tree to see what he could do. He decided to make the tree into a trough to feed his pigs. When his pigs began to eat from the trough, made from the tree that grew from his father's grave, they got very big and very fat. One day, the older brother saw these pigs and asked, "How did your pigs get so fat?" The younger brother said, "I feed them from the trough I made from the tree that grew on our father's grave." The older brother said, "I want fat pigs too; let me use your trough." The younger brother let him take the trough, but warned him to use it only three times, or something bad would happen again. The first time the older brother fed his pigs from the trough, they grew bigger. The second time, they grew even bigger. The third time, he filled the trough up with all the food he had, and the pigs ate so much that they blew up and died. The older brother was very angry, so he cut up the trough and burned it in his fireplace. Some days later, the younger brother came to get his trough. "It was no good," said the older brother. "My pigs ate from it and they died, so I burned it in my fireplace." The younger brother went to the fireplace, and he could find only one small piece of wood left from the trough. He took the piece of wood home to see what he could do with it.

The younger brother made a comb from the small piece of wood from the trough he had made from the tree that grew on his father's grave. Every time he used that comb, his hair got longer and more beautiful. One day, the older brother saw him and asked, "How did your hair get so long?" The younger brother showed him the comb and the older brother said, "Let me use it; I want long, beautiful hair too." The younger brother told him he could use it, but only three times, or something bad would happen again. The older brother took the comb home with him. The first time he used it, his hair grew longer; and the second time, it grew even longer. Then he said to his wife, "This is the third time. I will go up to the second floor and use the comb." But it pulled all of his hair out. The older brother was very angry and he threw the comb into the fire.

Later the younger brother came to get his comb. "It was no good," said the older brother, "see how it pulled out my hair. I threw it into the fire." The younger brother looked through the ashes, but all he could find was one tooth left from the comb that came from the trough, which he made from the tree that grew on his father's grave. He took that one tooth home and made it into a fishing hook. When he went to the river, each time he threw the hook into the water, he caught fish. He took all the fish home and was cooking them when his older brother came to visit. "Where did you get all those fish," he asked. The younger brother showed him the hook and said, "With this." "Let me use it," said the older brother, "I need fish too." The younger brother said he could use it, but only three times; if he used it more, something very bad would happen.

The older brother went to the river; the first time he used the hook, he caught fish; the second time he caught more fish. Then he said, "This is the third time. I will throw the hook far out into the middle of the river and catch the largest fish there." The older brother cast the hook into the middle of the river. He caught something, but it was too strong for him to pull it in. He tried and tried and finally gave up, leaving the hook there. When the younger brother came to get his hook back, the older brother said, "It was no good. I threw it into the middle of the river, but it got caught there, so I left it." The younger brother was very sad, so he went to the river and sat there for three days, thinking about what he should do.

On the third day, a beautiful woman walked up out of the river and said to the younger brother, "My father is the dragon that lives in the river, and he is very sick. Will you come and help him?" The younger brother said, "I can't go into the river; I wouldn't be able to breathe." The woman said, "Come with me." She put his head under her arm and he could see and breathe as they went to her father's house in the middle of the river. Her father and his brother were waiting for them, and the younger brother said to the dragon, "What's wrong with you?" The dragon answered, "I have a terrible pain in my throat." The dragon's brother said, "If you can help my brother, you will be able to choose your own reward. You can have wealth and riches or you may marry my brother's daughter." The younger brother looked into the dragon's throat and saw the hook which he had made from the comb that came from the trough that he had made from the tree that grew on his father's grave. He reached into the dragon's throat and moved the hook just a little bit. The dragon said it felt better, and the younger brother promised to come back and do a little more each day.

For nine days, the younger brother stayed at the dragon's house in the middle of the river. Each day, he moved the hook just a little bit, and each day he spent more time with the dragon's beautiful daughter. On the last day, she said, "I know you will cure my father and his brother will offer you a reward. Please do not take wealth and riches; please choose to marry me." That day the younger brother removed the hook from the dragon's throat, and the dragon was healed. "Now," said the dragon's brother, "you may choose your reward. Will you take great wealth and riches, or will you marry my brother's daughter?" The younger brother and the dragon's daughter were married; they left her father's house and started their own family on the banks of the river.

The Older Brother and the Younger Brother
("Npawg hlub thiab npawg yau")

Once there were two brothers; the older brother was not married, but the younger brother was. One day the older brother said to the younger brother, "I have heard there is work to be found building a new road; and maybe there will be new wives to be found, too." So the two brothers went off to work on the road and left the younger brother's wife behind. They worked hard all day, for many days. One day the older brother sneaked off and went back home to steal the younger brother's wife. The younger brother did not know he had left, so he worked all day long and far into the night. When it was midnight, he could not find his brother and he did not know the way home. Nearby he found a house with a mother tiger at home. She said he could sleep upstairs, so he climbed the ladder and went to bed.

The mother tiger's three sons came home later that night. The first son brought a cow; the second brought a deer and the third brought a pig. When the sons sat down in the house, they smelled something funny. When they asked what it was, their mother said it was their cousin who had come to visit. "Where is this cousin?" said the three sons, "bring him down so we can see him" The mother went up and brought the younger brother down. They could see he was not their cousin, so the three tigers began to question where he had come from and why he was there. The younger brother told the story of what had happened and how he was lost in the forest and could not find his way home. The tigers decided to have some fun with him, so they told him, "It is very dangerous for you in this forest all alone. We have neighbors who are mean and dangerous; they will kill and eat you if you are not careful." "What can I do?" asked the younger brother. The tigers told him, "Tomorrow, we will take you out into the forest and you will fight with us. If you can beat us, then we will know you are strong enough to protect yourself from our neighbors."

Now the tigers really wanted to kill the young man themselves, but he believed they wished to help him. The next day he went with them far out into the forest and they fought. The tigers thought they would beat him easily, but the young man was too strong for them. "Well," said the tigers, "you are very strong and it seems our neighbors will not be able to kill you and eat you." As a prize for passing this test, the tigers gave the young man a knife.

When they got back home, the tigers tried one more test to trick the young man. "You still might not be strong enough to beat our neighbors," they said. "Let us test your strength with a pig. We will each kill and prepare a pig for cooking. If you lose this test, surely our neighbors will be able to kill you and eat you." So they all killed pigs and prepared them for cooking, but the young man won that test too. The tigers were upset, but they had to admit the young man was too strong for them. As a prize for winning this test, they gave him another knife, a cow and some money. Then they showed him the way home and sent him safely on his way.

When the younger brother got home, he found that his older brother had taken his wife away. But he had enough riches from the tigers to find himself a new wife.

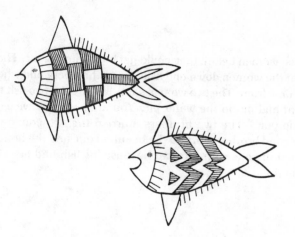

The Two Brothers and the Fish
("Ob kwv tij thiab ntses")

Once there were two orphan brothers who always went fishing together. One day each of the brothers caught a fish. The first brother started a fire and put his fish on it to cook. The other brother said, "I do not think we should cook these fish." The first brother took his fish off the fire and said, "All right, we will not cook them." When the two brothers got home, they put their fish in a large jar of water.

The next day the two brothers went to work in the fields. When they came home, they found a meal prepared and waiting for them. They ate the food; then they went to their neighbors to thank them for bringing dinner. All their neighbors said, "Are you crazy? We did not take any food to your house." No one could tell the brothers who had prepared the meal for them, so they went to the village "saub" to find out. The two brothers said, "We are very poor and do not have much good food. How is it that today we came home and found a good meal cooked and waiting for us? Our neighbors all say none of them did it." The "saub" said, "Go back home and hide in your house all day tomorrow; then you will find out who is doing this."

So the two brothers hid in their house the next day, and they saw two young women come out of the water jar. One of the women had a very beautiful face, but the other had a scar on her face. The brothers jumped out from their hiding place and caught the two women before they could get back into the jar. The brothers sat the women down and asked who they were and where they had come from. The two women said, "We are the two fish that you caught and put in the water jar. You are poor and we were sent to help you." The two brothers married the two young women; the second brother married the beautiful one and the first brother married the one with the scar because his fish had been scarred by the fire.

The Dragon and the Two Brothers
("Zag thiab ob kwv tij")

One day, two brothers were going home from the fields. As they walked along the road, they saw a beautiful young woman and an old man walking to the edge of the river. When the two brothers got home, they told their mother what they had seen and asked her who the beautiful woman and the old man were. Their mother told them not to talk to anyone about what they had seen or there would be trouble. When the brothers asked why they should keep it a secret, their mother told them that two people had come looking for the king's daughter who had been taken away by a dragon. The two brothers thought about this; then they went to find the people from the king.

When the two brothers told about the woman they had seen, the people from the king said, "That was the king's daughter. The old man with her was not an old man, but a dragon. If one of you would rescue her from this dragon, the king will allow you to marry her." The two brothers went to the edge of the river where they had seen the young woman and the old man. They found a cave that went down into the ground and they climbed down on a rope to look for the king's daughter. They found her sitting on a rock, sewing a tapestry, and they told her they had come to save her from the dragon. She said, "The dragon is too big; you will not be able to kill him. Come and see." She took them to a large field where the dragon slept, and the dragon filled up the whole field.

The brothers had brought only a knife to kill the dragon, but when they saw how large it was, both of them were afraid. The older brother said to the younger brother, "This young woman is so beautiful, it is only right that you should be the one to marry her. You take the knife and kill the dragon." The younger brother said, "Oh, no! You are the oldest, so you should marry this beautiful young woman. I will let you kill the dragon." "No," said the older brother, "I could not take her away from you. You may kill the dragon so you can marry this beautiful young woman." Finally, the younger brother took the knife and was able to kill the dragon.

The two brothers then took the king's daughter back to their rope to climb out of the cave. The older brother climbed up first; then the young woman went up, with the younger brother right behind her. As the woman climbed out of the cave, the older brother saw again how beautiful she was, and he wanted to marry her himself. As he helped her up, he took out his knife and cut the rope before his brother reached the top. As the younger brother fell back into the cave, he tried to hold onto the woman's shirt, but it tore and he fell to the bottom with the piece of cloth in his hand. The older brother went off to marry the king's daughter, leaving his younger brother behind in the cave.

The younger brother was in the cave for a long time and he got very hungry, so he went back to the dead dragon and ate it. Then he got very thirsty, so he began to dig into the walls of the cave to find water. As he was digging, he heard a voice in the wall, asking for help. The younger brother listened, then he asked, "Who is there?" The voice said, "I am Thunder. If you will help me get out of the wall, I will help you." The younger brother asked, "How did you get in there?" "The dragon took me from the sky and trapped me here," said Thunder, "Please help me." So the younger brother dug out the wall of the cave and set Thunder free.

Thunder said, "How can I help you?" The younger brother told Thunder he was very thirsty, so Thunder rolled and made it rain and the brother could drink all he wanted. Then the younger brother told Thunder what had happened and asked, "Can you get us out of this cave?" Thunder said, "Yes; if we walk, it will take three months. If we fly, it will take three days." The younger brother said, "I would like to find my brother and the king's daughter soon, but I cannot fly." Thunder said, "Do not worry, I will help you fly." Thunder put the younger brother's head under his arm and they flew out of the cave together.

When they got to the king's house, the older brother had already married the king's daughter. The younger brother went to the king and told him what happened. "I killed the dragon," he said, "so I should marry your daughter." The king said, "Now I will decide. One of you has a piece of cloth from my daughter's shirt. That one will marry her." The older brother showed the king an old piece of cloth he had, but it was not the same as the daughter's shirt. The younger brother took out the piece of cloth he had torn from her shirt as he fell into the cave. The king looked at it and said, "This is the right piece. You are the one who will marry my daughter."

The Three Brothers

There once was a king who was very good at finding the right place to bury people. (The Hmong people believe that it brings good fortune to find the best place to bury a relative, especially parents.) The king had three sons, and they worried about what would happen when their father died. He was good at finding the right place to bury others, but who could find the right place to bury him? The king told his sons, "Do not worry; I will live to be one hundred years old. When I die, you will tie up my body and carry me until the rope breaks. In that place, you will bury me."

The king did live to be one hundred years old. When he died, his sons tied up his body and carried him many miles, through three different countries. When they came to a place where nine roads came together, the rope broke, and they buried their father in that place. After that, the three brothers went to three different countries to study, and they stayed for three years. When the first brother was returning home, he came to the intersection of nine roads, and he met his two brothers, who were also returning home. The three brothers sat down to talk about what they had learned during the past three years.

The first brother said, "For three years, I studied how to clap my hands and stamp my feet, and then fly away to the ends of the earth." The second brother said, "For three years, I studied the words to speak to make people die and the words to speak to make them come alive again." The third brother said, "For three years, I studied how to speak with the animals." As the three brothers sat and talked, a flock of birds flew over their heads. The second brother said to the third brother, "You know how to speak with animals; tell us what those birds are saying." The third brother answered, "They are talking about a country where all the animals have died and there is plenty of flesh to eat." The second brother said to the first brother, "You know how to make us fly; take us to see this country." So the first brother clapped his hands and stamped his feet, and the three brothers flew off to see the country where all the animals had died.

The king of that country had a very special horse, which had died with all the other animals. When the three brothers saw this horse, the first brother said to the second brother, "You know how to bring the dead back to life; do this for the king's horse." So the second brother spoke and the king's horse came back to life. When the horse ran back to the king's house, the king was happy and surprised. He said to one of his soldiers, "Go quickly and find out who has brought my horse back to life." The soldier looked where the horse had been and he found only the three brothers. When he told this to the king, the king said, "Bring the three brothers to me." When the brothers came to the king, he asked, "Did you bring my horse back to life?" The second brother said, "Yes, I know how to speak and make things die and how to speak and bring them back to life."

The king laughed and said, "Do you expect me to believe that you can make things die and come back to life again?" The second brother said, "Yes. The king will die." At that moment the king died. Then the second brother said, "The king will live again." At that moment, the king came back to life. And the king believed. He decided that the three brothers could rule much better than he could, so he made them kings in his place.

The Father and His Three Sons
("Leej txiv thiab nws peb tug tub")

There was once a man with three sons, and he told them all
to go and find jobs to support him. The first son went north, the
second son went south, and the third son went east. The first two
sons found jobs, worked very hard for a long time, and made a
great deal of money. The third son worked a little bit; mostly he
gambled and lost all of his money. All three sons stayed away from
home for a long time. When the third son was ready to return to
his father, the man he was staying with asked him to sweep the
floor. In payment for this, he gave the third son a jar and told him,
"If your brothers treat you well when you see them, you will not
need to open this jar. If they try to hurt you, open the jar and it
will help you."

On his way home, the third son saw his two brothers on the
road, bringing home money, cows, pigs and horses. When the two
brothers saw that the third son was bringing nothing home, the
oldest brother said, "You have not done enough to support our
father." Then he hit the third son and knocked him down, and
the other two left him there to go home to their father. When the
third son woke up, he remembered what the man had told him.
He opened up his jar and money and animals came out of it. He
got on the horse and rode after his brothers. When he caught up
with his brothers, he rode very fast past the oldest brother and
knocked him down. When he got ahead of them, he went off to

the side of the road, put all the money and animals back in the jar, and waited for his brothers to pass by.

After they passed, he followed and caught up with them. When his oldest brother saw him, he said, "You saw that man on the horse who rode by and knocked me down, but you did not help me." The oldest brother hit him again and knocked him down, and the two brothers went on into the town. When they reached town, they went to a very rich merchant to sell all their goods, so they would have enough money to support their father. The rich man took their goods, but he said he could not pay them until the next day. When the third son found them the next day, they were still waiting to be paid. The following day the rich man returned with a big knife and said, "If you can break this knife, I will pay you. I will come back tomorrow to see how you have done."

When the rich man left, the oldest brother tried to break the knife, but he could not. The second brother tried, but he could not break it either. When they asked the third son to help them, he said, "Why should I help you after you have treated me so badly?" All night, the two older brothers tried to break the knife, but they could not. Finally, the next day, the third brother agreed to help them, and together, they broke it. When the rich man returned, he was surprised that the knife was broken, but he had to pay the brothers, and they could finally go home.

When they got to their father's house, they told him everything that had happened. The two older brothers offered the money they had, but the third son opened his jar and offered his father the animals that were inside. The father thought the animals were better support than money, so he told the two older brothers that his third son knew much better how to support him and from now on, they would take their orders from him.